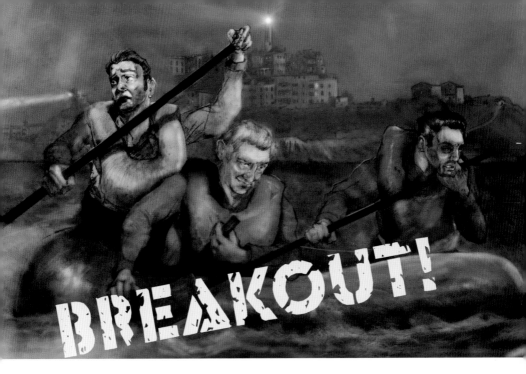

BREAKOUT!

ESCAPE FROM ALCATRAZ

By Lori Haskins Houran

Illustrated by Dave Norton

GOLDEN GATE NATIONAL PARKS CONSERVANCY
SAN FRANCISCO, CALIFORNIA

Golden Gate National Parks Conservancy
Building 201 Fort Mason,
San Francisco, California 94123
www.parksconservancy.org

Photographs courtesy Golden Gate National Recreation Area/Park Archives
and Records Center unless otherwise noted.
This book was originally published by Random House/Books for Young Readers

ISBN 978-1-932519-23-5
Library of Congress Control Number: 2012945014

Development: Robert Lieber
Illustrations: Dave Norton
Design: Vivian Young
Editor: Susan Tasaki
Alcatraz Subject Specialist: John Moran
Production: Sarah Lau Levitt

Printed in the USA on recycled paper

www.nps.gov/alcatraz

PARKS FOR ALL FOREVER™

THE ESCAPE
June 11, 1962, 9:30 PM
United States Penitentiary
Alcatraz Island

It is dark inside the prison walls. Four men in four separate cells lie still, waiting.

"Sixteen, seventeen, eighteen . . ."

The men hear the guard coming down the hall. The guard is taking a head count. He is counting the prisoners to make sure they are all in their beds.

"Nineteen, twenty, twenty-one . . ."

The men close their eyes and pretend to be asleep. But they are not going to sleep tonight.

Tonight, they are going to escape!

The guard walks past the cell of Clarence Anglin, a bank robber. In the next cell is his brother, John. John Anglin is a bank robber, too.

"Twenty-two, twenty-three . . ."

The guard keeps walking. Four doors down is a car thief named Allen West. And next to him is Frank Lee Morris, another bank robber.

All four of the men have tried to escape from prisons before. That is why they were sent to Alcatraz. Alcatraz is the toughest maximum-security prison in the world. Some say it is even escape-proof.

What makes Alcatraz so tough? There are head counts all day and all night. There are high barbed-wire fences around the prison walls. There are high towers in the prison yard where guards with searchlights and rifles keep careful watch over the prison. Most important of all, there is the bay.

This federal penitentiary sits on the tiny island of Alcatraz, in the middle of San Francisco Bay. The water in the bay is very cold, and the currents are dangerously swift. In just seconds, the water can numb a swimmer's arms and legs, and the currents can suck him under.

The men know this. They know that most people believe it is impossible to escape from Alcatraz. But they are going to try.

"Twenty-eight, twenty-nine . . ."

The men wait until the guard has passed by. Then, one by one, they slip out of bed and sneak to the back of their cells.

In the rear wall of each cell at Alcatraz, near the floor, is an air vent: a small hole covered by a metal grate. One night, a year ago, West peered through the grate and saw a hallway full of pipes. Some of the pipes ran straight up to the cellhouse roof!

West was excited. If he could get to that hallway, he could make it outside. But how was he going to fit through the vent? It was only ten inches wide and six inches high—roughly the size of a shoebox cover. And it was surrounded by a thick concrete wall.

West examined the concrete wall closely. The concrete was hard, but West could see that it was starting to crack and crumble in places. The prison was so old that the walls were beginning to rot.

West smiled. He knew what he was going to do. He was going to dig a hole right through the wall. He was going to turn his air vent into an escape tunnel!

West told John Anglin, Clarence Anglin, and Frank Lee Morris about his plan. He asked them if they wanted to go along. The three men said yes.

That June, they began to dig. It was slow going. They used sharpened spoon handles and other homemade tools to chip through the concrete. They worked at night and had to be quiet so the guards wouldn't hear them. And every time a guard came by, they had to cover the holes back up and creep into bed for the head count.

Finally, after nine months, the tunnels were nearly ready. But the men could not break out yet. They had a problem. What were they going to do about the head counts on the night of the escape? As soon as the guard noticed they were missing, he would sound the alarm. They wouldn't have enough time to get away.

Then Clarence had a clever idea. He took the crumbled concrete from the walls and mixed it with soap and water to make plaster. He molded the plaster into four heads. Then he painted faces on the heads and glued on hair stolen from the prison barbershop.

The dummy heads were crude. But in the dark, they might just be good enough to fool the guards.

Now the men had another problem to solve. An even bigger problem. How were they going to get across the bay? They needed a boat. And they were going to have to make it themselves.

Alcatraz issued each prisoner a rubber raincoat along with his prison clothes. John Anglin and Allen West

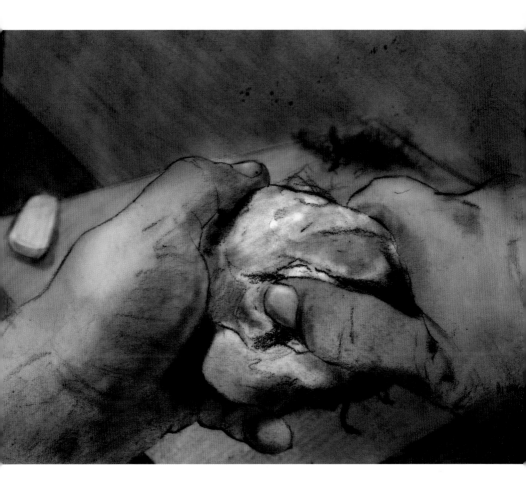

borrowed as many raincoats as they could from the other
prisoners. They cut the raincoats into pieces and sewed
the pieces together in the shape of a raft. They sealed
the edges of the raft by pressing them against a hot pipe.
Then they took the leftover pieces of rubber and made
life jackets the same way.

Meanwhile, Morris got hold of a concertina. A
concertina is a musical instrument that works like an

accordion. When it is squeezed, it produces a strong current of air.

Morris took the keys off the concertina so that it wouldn't make any noise. Now they could use the concertina to inflate the raft. To steer the raft, they would use paddles made out of the wooden shelves in their cells.

The men had no way of knowing if the raft would really work. Would the air stay inside it? Would it hold the weight of the four men?

The night of the escape—tonight—would be the only test.

Shortly after 9:30 PM, the men reach into the air-vent tunnels and take out their dummy heads. They place the heads on their pillows and pull the blankets snugly around them.

The men rush back to the air vents. The Anglins and Morris crawl through their tunnels into the hallway. They wait for West to crawl through, too. But he doesn't appear.

Seconds tick by. Where is West?

Morris leans down to West's air vent. "What are you doing?" he whispers. "We have to go!"

West whispers back. His voice is frantic. "I can't get through the hole!"

West had been impatient when he was digging his tunnel. He knew he had an inch or so to go, but he thought he could kick the last few pieces out on the night of the escape. Now he sees something he never noticed before: an iron bar running alongside the air vent!

"You guys have to help me break this bar!" he whispers.

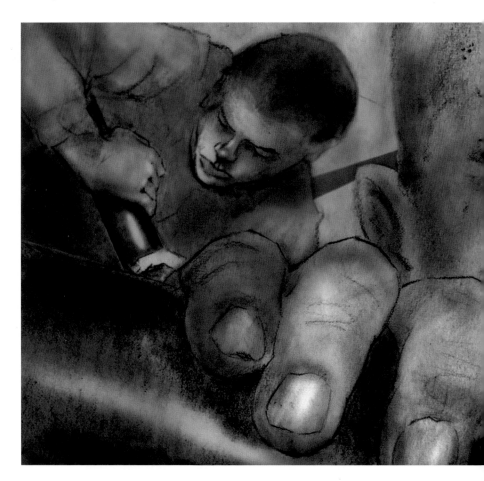

Morris and the Anglin brothers look at each other. They know that time is precious. The faster they get out, the better their chances of survival.

The three men make a decision. They decide to go— without West.

Morris and the Anglins quickly climb the pipes to the top of the cellhouse, where they have hidden the life jackets, the raft, the concertina, and the paddles. They leave West's life jacket and paddle behind.

In the roof above them is a vent crisscrossed with iron bars. While West and John Anglin were making the rafts and the life jackets, Morris and Clarence Anglin had been sawing through the bars. Now all they have to do is push open the vent and they will see the moon!

Morris gives the vent a shove. It falls on the roof with a loud clang!

The men freeze. They expect to hear the sound of running footsteps below them and the shrill ring of the escape alarm.

But all is silent.

The men sneak across the roof and shinny down a pipe on the side of the building, carrying their equipment with them.

As soon as they hit the ground, they start running. They scramble over the barbed-wire fences and race to the shore. Lucky for them, the nearby guard tower is empty.

The men quickly inflate the life jackets and the raft. Then they stand for a moment at the water's edge. Across the bay, more than a mile away, they can see the lights of San Francisco glimmering.

Freedom!

The three men grab their paddles, climb aboard the raft, and push off into the cold, whirling waters of the bay.

THE SEARCH
June 12, 1962, 7:15 AM

"**R**ise and shine. Let's go, everybody."

Officer Bartlett strides down the hall, counting the sleepy prisoners standing at the front of their cells.

Halfway down the hall, Bartlett stops outside John Anglin's cell. Anglin is still in bed.

"Come on. You're late for head count," says Bartlett. Anglin doesn't move.

Bartlett frowns. "Wake up!" Anglin still doesn't move.

Bartlett calls Officer Long over.

"I got one I can't get awake," Bartlett tells him.

"I'll wake him up," grumbles Long. He reaches into Anglin's cell and taps him on the head. To his surprise, Anglin's head rolls off the pillow and onto the floor!

"It's a dummy!" Long shouts.

He looks in the cell next door. Sure enough, there's a dummy in Clarence Anglin's bed, too. And down the hall, there's one on Frank Lee Morris's pillow.

Long sounds the escape alarm. Another officer calls Arthur Dollison, the acting warden, and tells him what's happened. Dollison instructs the guards to search every inch of the island.

The guards look everywhere. The missing prisoners are nowhere to be found. But on top of the cellhouse, the guards discover a homemade life jacket and paddle. And in one of the cells, they find a November 1960 issue of *Popular Mechanics* magazine, with an article that shows how to make a raft! Could the convicts have made it off the island?

Dollison immediately contacts the Coast Guard, the Navy, the California Highway Patrol, and the FBI. A massive manhunt begins.

Coast Guard crews investigate every cave and cove on Alcatraz and the nearby islands. Navy divers search for clues underwater. Ordinary citizens join in, too. They comb the beaches of San Francisco looking for traces of the three men.

The California Highway Patrol puts out an All-Points Bulletin, warning police officers to keep an eye out for the escapees. And the FBI questions everyone inside and outside Alcatraz who might know something about the escape.

The person they question the closest is Allen West. West admits right away that he was involved. "You might as well throw me in the Hole," he says. "I planned the entire escape."

West brags about the breakout to the FBI. But when they ask him what Morris and the Anglins were planning to do once they got off the island, West suddenly gets hazy. He says he isn't sure—he thinks they were going to

steal some money and some guns, then split up. The FBI is certain West knows more. But he isn't telling.

Meanwhile, the search goes on. The first night, a homemade paddle is found floating in the bay. It matches the one on top of the cellhouse.

Three days later, a plastic pouch floats to the surface. The pouch contains the addresses of the Anglin brothers' friends and relatives! The FBI contacts them all. No one has heard from the missing brothers.

Over the next two weeks, more evidence washes ashore. First one of the life jackets. Then pieces of the raft.

Prison officials become convinced that the three men

drowned. They think the raft sank, and the paddle and the pouch went overboard. They think the men tried to swim to shore, but the life jackets didn't work.

But not everyone is convinced. Some people think the escapees might still be alive. What if they made it to shore, then threw the evidence into the water to make it look as if they drowned?

Weeks pass. The Coast Guard continues to search the bay, waiting for the bodies to surface. But they never do. Frank Lee Morris and the Anglin brothers have disappeared.

Did the three men drown? Did they make it? No one knows for sure. But one thing is certain—the escape-proof prison is not escape-proof anymore.

Nine months after the breakout, the United States Attorney General orders Alcatraz closed. The breakout is not the only reason. Another reason is money; the government decides that Alcatraz is too expensive to run.

Alcatraz officials begin sending the inmates to other prisons.

On March 21, 1963, the final twenty-seven prisoners are marched off the island in handcuffs and shackles. They are the last men ever to serve time on Alcatraz.

THEN: THE DIRTY THIRTIES

Doc Barker,
Bank Robber,
Kidnapper,
Murderer

Bernie Coy,
Bank Robber

Machine Gun Kelly,
Kidnapper

U. S. PENITENTIARY
ALCATRAZ
415

1 1 7

U. S. PENITENTI
ALCATRAZ
268

AL CAPONE, CHICAGO GANGSTER

If Morris and the Anglin brothers made it, they were the first men ever to successfully break out of Alcatraz. In twenty-nine years, not one prisoner was known to have escaped from Alcatraz alive.

The prison opened in 1934, during the decade called the "Dirty Thirties." Why were the 1930s so dirty? A crime wave was sweeping America. Every day, the newspapers were full of stories about armed robberies, kidnappings, and murders.

Many of the crimes were committed by gangsters—criminals who banded together in powerful gangs. It was hard to catch the gangsters. They had more money, more men, and more guns than the police!

Even if a gangster was sent to jail, he wouldn't always stay there. Sometimes the other members of his gang would "spring" him. They would come to the prison armed with machine guns and break out the gangster! The next day, the gangster would be back on the street, committing more crimes.

Americans were afraid. They were also angry. Why weren't these criminals stopped?

J. Edgar Hoover, the young director of the FBI, was determined to clean up the Dirty Thirties. He wanted to put the gangsters behind bars for good. But how?

Hoover came up with the idea for a "super prison." Only the worst criminals would be sent there. It would be the strictest, toughest prison in the world. And it would be one hundred percent escape-proof.

Hoover and the Justice Department set about looking for a site for the super prison. They wanted a place that was remote, or difficult to reach. They figured the harder the prison was to get to, the harder it would be to escape from.

They looked all over the country—in the far-off corners of Alaska, in the middle of the Nevada desert. None of the places seemed right.

Then they heard about Alcatraz, a tiny island in the middle of San Francisco Bay. It was a twenty-two-acre hunk of solid rock, separated from the nearest land by more than a mile of treacherous waters.

Alcatraz was perfect. There was even a jail on the island already! The jail belonged to the Army. They had been sending disorderly soldiers and prisoners of war there for more than seventy years. But now they were preparing to shut it down.

The Justice Department asked the Army to turn Alcatraz over to them, and the Army agreed. It was official: Alcatraz would become the home of the new super prison.

The Justice Department spent hundreds of thousands of dollars turning Alcatraz from an Army jail into a maximum-security prison.

They replaced the soft iron bars on the cells with unbreakable hardened steel ones. They installed metal detectors in the hallways. They put up barbed-wire fences and guard towers. They posted signs around the island that said:

WARNING!
UNITED STATES PENITENTIARY
BOATS MUST KEEP OFF 200 YARDS

The Justice Department chose a man named James A. Johnston to be the warden, or head, of the prison. Then they hired one hundred highly trained officers to guard it. Finally, everything was ready.

On August 11, 1934, United States Penitentiary Alcatraz Island opened its doors to America's most dangerous and cunning convicts.

JAMES A. JOHNSTON

HARD TIME:
ALCATRAZ PRISON LIFE

John Louie

Warden Johnston let the convicts know right away that life on Alcatraz was not going to be easy.

They could have only one visitor a month. All their mail would be opened by prison officials. They would not be allowed to read any newspapers or magazines, or to listen to the radio. They would not even be allowed to talk to each other!

Each prisoner was assigned a cell. Each cell was five feet wide and nine feet long. Inside were a bed, two shelves, a toilet, and a sink.

Three times a day, the convicts were marched to the dining hall for meals. Twice a week, they were marched to the bathing room for showers. The rest of the time, they were locked in their cells.

Imagine what it would be like to spend a whole day locked in a room with nothing to do and nobody to talk to. Now imagine sitting in that room for two days. Or three. Or four.

The prisoners at Alcatraz were not just there for a few days. Some faced ten-year sentences. Some faced twenty- or thirty-year sentences. Others were locked up for life!

If a prisoner was well behaved, he could earn a few privileges. He could get a job working in the kitchen, the laundry room, or one of the prison factories. Once a

week, he could go outside to the exercise yard. There, he could play games, sit in the sun, and talk with the other prisoners.

But if the convict was caught breaking prison rules, he would lose his privileges. And if he did something serious—if he started a fight or attacked a guard—he would be sent to the Hole.

The Hole was a row of cells set aside for punishment. Each door in the Hole was made of solid steel. Once the door was closed, the cell was pitch-black inside. The prisoner couldn't see anything. He couldn't hear anything. The only contact he had with another person was when a guard pushed his food through a narrow slot in the door.

Prisoners sometimes spent weeks in the Hole, sitting in the dark. The loneliness was terrible. Some men cried. Others screamed or beat their fists against the wall.

As stories about life at Alcatraz reached the outside world, Americans became divided. Some people supported the prison's tough measures. After all, the prisoners there had committed awful crimes. Why shouldn't they be treated harshly?

But other people were not so sure. They worried that Alcatraz wasn't helping criminals mend their ways. Instead, it was only making them more hardened and more hateful.

Over the years, Alcatraz changed. The no-talking rule was abolished. The prisoners were allowed to have radios and magazines in their cells. Some were allowed to paint or play musical instruments.

But life on Alcatraz was still tough. The convicts described the prison as a hard, hopeless place. They called it the Rock. Hellcatraz. The Island of the Living Dead.

Nearly all of the prisoners thought about escaping. But few dared to try. Between 1934 and 1961, there were twelve escape attempts. Some of the escapees were shot. Some were captured. Some drowned. None of them made it.

Until 1962, J. Edgar Hoover's super prison lived up to its name.

PRISON CELLBLOCK

PRISON DINING HALL

PRISON LAUNDRY

PRISON LIBRARY

NOW: A TRIP TO THE ROCK

Mike Long

It is almost fifty years later. A ferry pulls up to the dock at Alcatraz. One by one, passengers step off the ferry and onto the island.

The passengers don't have handcuffs around their wrists or shackles around their ankles. Instead, they have cameras around their necks. They are tourists, and they have come to see the most legendary prison in American history: Alcatraz.

The people climb the steep concrete steps to the prison. They are laughing and talking in the cool morning air. But as they enter the cellhouse, they suddenly grow quiet.

The visitors walk slowly through the halls, staring into each cell. What was it like to live in one of the tiny rooms for ten or twenty years?

A few of the cell doors are open. Some of the people step inside. They wrap their hands around the cold metal bars. A chill runs up their spines. They can imagine the heavy metal doors clanging shut, locking them in.

The visitors keep walking. They pass the Hole. They pass the dining hall. On the wall is the breakfast menu for March 21, 1963—Alcatraz's last day as a federal penitentiary.

Around the corner, a crowd gathers outside one of

the cells. For a moment, it appears as if a man is lying in the bed! But on closer look, it is not a man after all. It is a dummy.

Next to the cell is a picture of three men: Frank Lee Morris, John Anglin, and Clarence Anglin. Beneath the picture is a description of their bold breakout on June 11, 1962.

FRANK MORRIS   JOHN ANGLIN   CLARENCE ANGLIN

The tourists all ask each other the same question: *Do you think they made it?*

Do you?

More Alcatraz Stories for Younger Readers

Al Capone Does My Shirts, by Gennifer Choldenko
(New York: Putnam, 2004. Ages 10 and up. Fiction)
When twelve-year-old Moose Flannagan's father gets a new job and moves his family to Alcatraz Island in 1935, Moose isn't entirely happy. Not only do his schoolmates think he's weird for living on the island, his new neighbors—some of America's most dangerous criminals—leave something to be desired.

Al Capone Shines My Shoes, by Gennifer Choldenko
(New York: Dial, 2009. Ages 10 and up. Fiction)
In this sequel, Moose thinks that Al Capone has engineered his sister's acceptance into a special school in San Francisco. Now, Moose owes Capone—or does he?

The Children of Alcatraz: Growing Up on the Rock, by Claire Rudolf Murphy
(New York: Walker Books, 2006. Ages 8 and up. Nonfiction)
Talk about one-of-a-kind childhoods! Filled with archival and family photographs, this book profiles generations of children who grew up on "the Rock." Interviews, anecdotes, and historical documents round out the story.